Diagraming Sentences

BY
DEBORAH WHITE BROADWATER

COPYRIGHT © 2004 Mark Twain Media, Inc.

ISBN   10-digit: 1-58037-282-1
13-digit: 978-1-58037-282-4

Printing No. CD-404008

Mark Twain Media, Inc., Publishers
Distributed by Carson-Dellosa Publishing Company, Inc.

Table of Contents

Introduction

Students have not had the opportunity to diagram sentences in classrooms for several years. Diagraming sentences is a process that helps students to see how the parts of speech go together to make a complete sentence and to see what might be missing from the sentence. This is extremely helpful to those who are visual learners.

Diagraming sentences helps students work through a sentence when something doesn't sound right or look right. By creating a diagram, students are able to picture how the sentence is written.

This book starts from the beginning of sentence diagraming and shows the student how to diagram simple sentences with just a subject and a verb. It then progresses through adjectives and adverbs, all the way to compound sentences. There are explanations of how to draw the diagram for each part of speech and sentences to practice the skills. There are reviews after several lessons, which may be used as quizzes or tests.

This book is intended to offer both teachers and parents the opportunity to help the student improve his or her ability to diagram sentences. The pages may be copied so the student can keep them in a binder to use as a resource.

Teachers may use these activities when teaching vocabulary to the whole class as part of a writing workshop. They may also use these activities with students as remedial exercises.

Each unit can be used in order, or the units can be used in isolation.

Diagraming Subjects and Predicates

When diagraming sentences, the horizontal line under the subject and predicate is called the base line. The subject is written on the left side of the base line, and the predicate is on the right side of the base line. A vertical dividing line that crosses the base line is drawn between the subject and verb. Punctuation is not used in a sentence diagram.

Michael ate.   **Fish swim.**

| subject | verb | | Michael | ate | | Fish | swim |

Compound subjects are both written on the left side of the base line. The conjunction that connects the two subjects is written on a dotted line between the two subject lines.

Paul and Bill play.

Compound verbs are both written on the right side of the base line. The conjunction that connects the two verbs is written on a dotted line between the two verb lines.

Beth reads and writes.

Sentences with compound subjects and compound verbs have the subjects written on two lines on the left side of the base line, and the verbs are written on two lines on the right side of the base line. The conjunction that connects the two subjects is written on a dotted line between the two subjects, and the conjunction that connects the two verbs is written on a dotted line between the two verbs.

Andrew and Troy worked and played.

When the subject is understood, as in commands, it is written on the left side of the base line in parentheses.

Sit!

| (understood subject) | verb | | (you) | Sit |

Name: _____   Date: _____

Diagraming Subjects and Predicates: Practice Activity 1

Directions: Diagram the following sentences in the space provided. Use the correct form. An example is given.

1. Grass grows.	5. Jeff laughed and chuckled. Jeff | laughed / and / chuckled
2. Dogs play.	6. Caroline wrote and drew.
3. Cats and kittens purr.	7. Jeff and Marie sing and dance.
4. John and I raced.	8. Connor and Kelsey tried but lost.

Name: _____ Date: _____

Diagraming Subjects and Predicates: Practice Activity 2

Directions: Diagram the following sentences in the space provided. Use the correct form. An example is given.

1. Emily and Erica dance and sing.	5. She and I draw and paint.
2. Jamal skates.	6. Mother washes and dries.
3. Alexis, Pam, and Li sang.	7. Elena will dance.
4. Charles and William will work.	8. Tigger jumped and slid.

4. Charles and William will work.

Charles
William
and
will work

Diagraming Adjectives, Adverbs, Direct Objects, Indirect Objects

When diagraming sentences, the adjective is written on a line under the word the adjective modifies. Articles are written on a line under the word to which they refer.

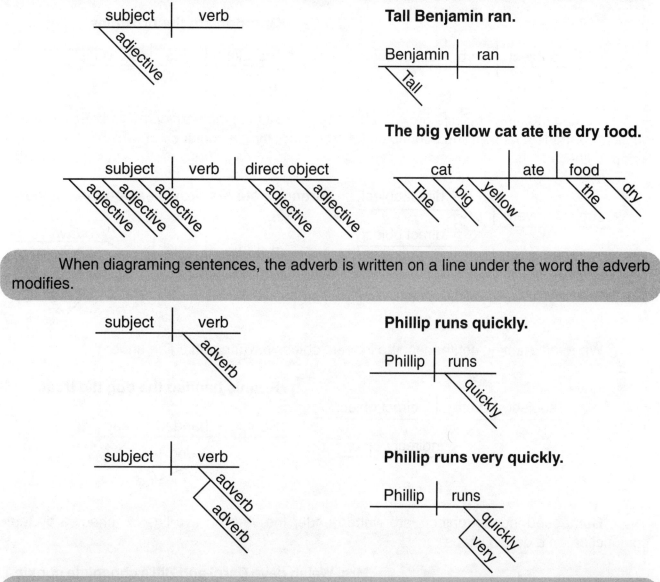

Tall Benjamin ran.

The big yellow cat ate the dry food.

When diagraming sentences, the adverb is written on a line under the word the adverb modifies.

Phillip runs quickly.

Phillip runs very quickly.

Compound adverbs are written under the word they modify, and the conjunction is written on a dotted line connecting them.

Caroline walked quickly but quietly.

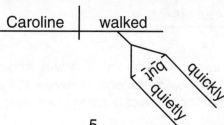

5

Diagraming Adjectives, Adverbs, Direct Objects, Indirect Objects (cont.)

When diagraming sentences, the direct object is written on the base line to the right of the verb. The dividing line does not cross the base line.

Compound direct objects are written on the base line to the right of the verb. Each direct object is written on its own line connected to each other by the conjunction, which is written on a dotted line.

When diagraming sentences, the indirect object is written on a line under the verb.

Compound indirect objects are written under the verb on two lines connected by the conjunction on a dotted line.

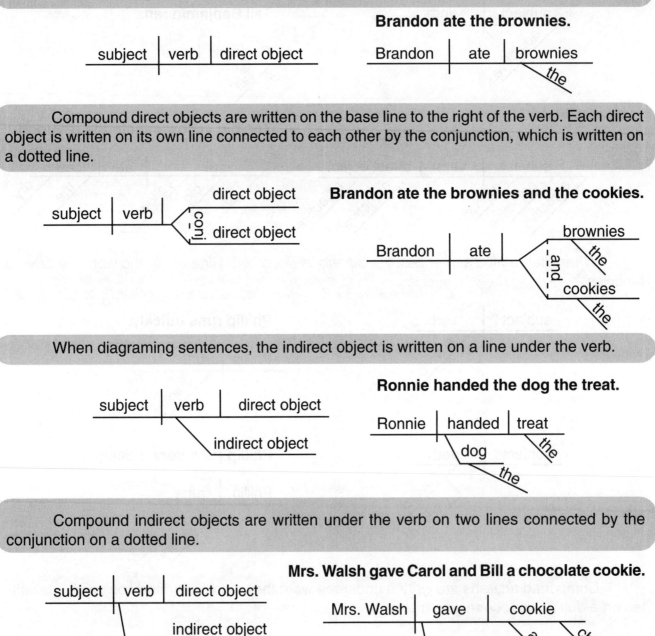

Teacher Note: Prepositional phrases, predicate nominatives, and predicate adjectives are used in some of the following exercises. You may want students to review the material on prepositional phrases on page 16 before beginning this section. Predicate nominatives and predicate adjectives are on page 26.

Name: _____ Date: _____

Diagraming Adjectives: Practice Activity

Directions: Diagram the following sentences in the space provided. Use the correct form. An example is given.

1. Joseph ate an apple. Joseph | ate | apple an	5. The beautiful white swans floated.
2. Kelsey rode the blue merry-go-round horse.	6. Randy owns a blue and white skateboard.
3. Sonja held my orange cat.	7. Did you eat the chocolate cake?
4. Hold the green water pitcher.	8. Dirty water filled the swimming pool.

Diagraming Adverbs: Practice Activity

Directions: Diagram the following sentences in the space provided. Use the correct form. An example is given.

1. Every student read quietly.	5. Josh and Ben worked quickly.
2. The sailboat glided very slowly.	6. Be very careful.
3. We drank the milkshake noisily.	7. Susan very quietly left the room.
4. Jan and Karen ran outside.	8. Did you open the box carefully?

For sentence 2, the diagram shows:

sailboat | glided

The (under sailboat), slowly (under glided), very (under slowly)

Name: _____   Date: _____

Diagraming Subjects, Predicates, Adjectives, Adverbs: Review Activity 1

Directions: Diagram the following sentences in the space provided. Use the correct form. An example is given.

1. Randy and Paul ate a huge dinner.	5. I quickly finished the essay question.
2. The big brown dog ran and jumped.	6. Did you open the door cautiously?
3. Karen really likes Lisa's sweater.	7. Yesterday we won our baseball game.
4. Todd and Curt painted the race car purple.	8. I happily ate the last chocolate chip cookie.

Name: _____ Date: _____

Diagraming Subjects, Predicates, Adjectives, Adverbs: Review Activity 2

Directions: Diagram the following sentences in the space provided. Use the correct form. An example is given.

1. The angry cat howled at the back door.	5. Louis won the speaking contest last year.
2. Jennifer and Katie sorted and tied the recycled newspapers.	6. Andrew and Carlos were absent yesterday and today.
3. Beth talks loudly.	7. Would you ask for help? you | Would ask for help
4. Please turn the pages carefully.	8. My sister and I share a small room.

Name: _____ Date: _____

Diagraming Direct Objects: Practice Activity 1

Directions: Diagram the following sentences in the space provided. Use the correct form. An example is given.

1. Mom made dinner.	5. Grandmother grows beautiful flowers.
2. The state has many parks. state | has | parks The / \ many	6. Alex and Clair are making a map.
3. Annie eats peanut butter and jelly.	7. Mrs. Evans collected the tests.
4. The snow covered the yards.	8. Rusty chased a rabbit.

Name: _____ Date: _____

Diagraming Direct Objects: Practice Activity 2

Directions: Diagram the following sentences in the space provided. Use the correct form. An example is given.

1. After the game, the pep club held a victory dance.	5. Ellen told David the story.
2. Harold drew a picture of the school.	6. During the hurricane, we lighted candles.
3. The cafeteria workers cleaned the kitchen.	7. William ate chips and cookies after school.
4. Laura read a book on the bus. Laura | read | book on bus / a the	8. Brandon asked Amy the question.

Name: _____ Date: _____

Diagraming Indirect Objects: Practice Activity

Directions: Diagram the following sentences in the space provided. Use the correct form. An example is given.

1. I wrote Lindsay a note.	5. Mrs. Manassah read the students a story in Spanish.
2. Ryan gave Paul a ride. Ryan | gave | ride / Paul / a	6. Aunt Betsy gave me a sweater for Christmas.
3. I bought Sarah a cookie at lunch.	7. Lavonne mailed Amber an invitation.
4. Jessica wrote our principal a note.	8. Wong prepared each of the baby birds food to eat.

Name: _____ Date: _____

Diagraming Subjects, Predicates, Adjectives, Adverbs, Direct Objects, Indirect Objects: Review Activity 1

Directions: Diagram the following sentences in the space provided. Use the correct form. An example is given.

1. What are you wearing to school tomorrow?	5. The pilot flew the plane to Hawaii.
2. Jake and I watched football yesterday.	6. Juan and Carol cleaned the band room.
3. Pepper caught the ball in the air.	7. The roofers nailed the shingles to the roof.
4. Who ate all of the cake?	8. All of the students took the history test.

14

Name: _____   Date: _____

Diagraming Subjects, Predicates, Adjectives, Adverbs, Direct Objects, Indirect Objects: Review Activity 2

Directions: Diagram the following sentences in the space provided. Use the correct form. An example is given.

1. Our neighbor gave me some flowers.	5. Alec wrote the governor a letter.
2. Mrs. Chen read the class a story about John Henry.	6. Dad and Ben cut and raked the yard.
3. Aunt Pat baked chocolate chip cookies for me.	7. Make the bed! (you) | Make | bed the
4. Dr. Adams filled my brother's tooth.	8. Blake played on the school baseball team.

Diagraming Prepositional Phrases

When diagraming sentences, the prepositional phrase is written below the word it modifies on a line with an extra extension. The object of the preposition is written on a horizontal line, and the adjectives used in the prepositional phrase are written on lines that come off the object's line.

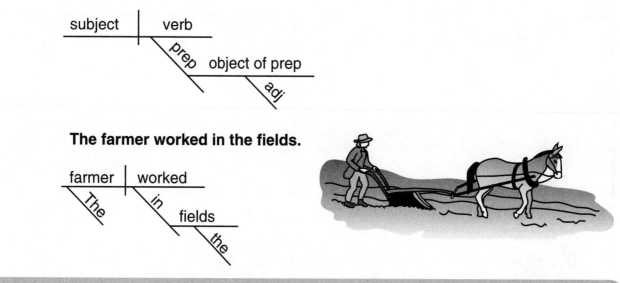

The farmer worked in the fields.

When diagraming a prepositional phrase that modifies another prepositional phrase, the first phrase is written off the word it modifies, and the second phrase is written off the word it modifies.

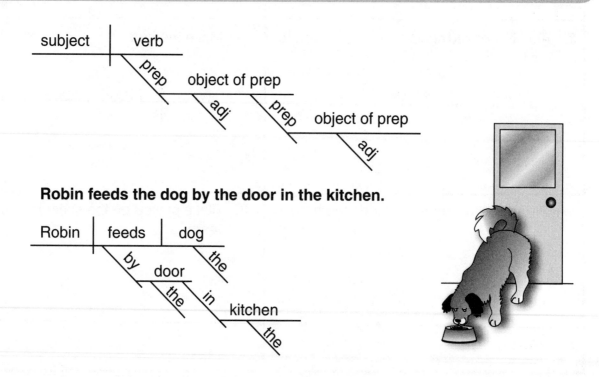

Robin feeds the dog by the door in the kitchen.

16

Diagraming Prepositional Phrases (cont.)

When diagraming sentences with prepositional phrases that have compound objects of a preposition, the compound objects are written on two lines coming off the preposition. A dotted line connects the two lines, and the conjunction is written on it.

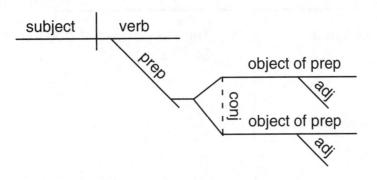

Astronomers look at the moon and stars.

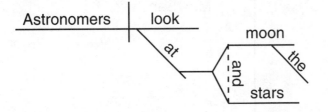

Name: _____ Date: _____

Diagraming Prepositional Phrases: Practice Activity 1

Directions: Diagram the following sentences in the space provided. Use the correct form. An example is given.

1. The dog ran across the backyard. dog | ran The / across backyard the	5. The train arrived at 7:00 P.M. from St. Louis.
2. Was that sandwich for me?	6. The cat on the chair is owned by Mrs. Sanchez.
3. The picnic basket was under the tree.	7. After a basket, the cheerleaders yell from the sidelines.
4. Connor dove into the swimming pool.	8. Whisper the secret in my ear.

Name: _____   Date: _____

Diagraming Prepositional Phrases: Practice Activity 2

Directions: Diagram the following sentences in the space provided. Use the correct form. An example is given.

1. The height of the bed frightened Sven.

2. The yards and trees were covered with snow after the blizzard.

3. Down in the basement behind the boxes hides the cat.

4. Lewis and Clark explored up the Missouri River.

5. The Masons went on their vacation without their dog.

6. After school, Mike raked the leaves in the yard.

Mike	raked	leaves

After | school · the · in yard · the

7. Six of my friends came to the party.

8. Mrs. Eitel's class won first prize in the contest.

Diagraming Participles, Gerunds, Infinitives

When diagraming sentences, the participle is written under the word it modifies. The participle is written in a curve, starting on the angled part of the line and continuing on the horizontal part of the line.

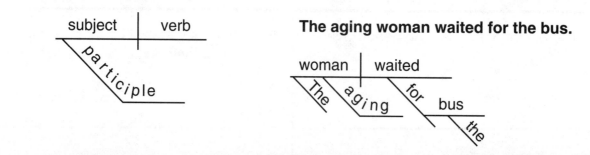

The aging woman waited for the bus.

When diagraming a participle phrase, the phrase is written under the word it modifies.

The yelling children burst into the room.

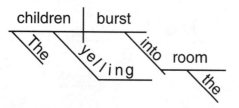

When diagraming sentences with gerunds, the gerund is written on a line and the object of the gerund (if there is one) is written after it, divided by a line like that of the direct object. The gerund is written in a curve around the right angle of the line. Since gerunds can be many parts of speech, this diagraming is placed in the part of speech.

Swimming is fun exercise.

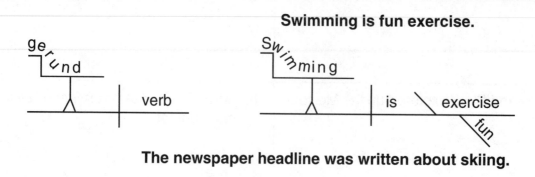

The newspaper headline was written about skiing.

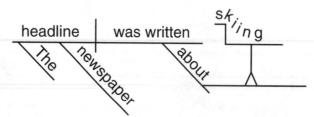

Diagraming Participles, Gerunds, Infinitives (cont.)

The team enjoys playing basketball every practice.

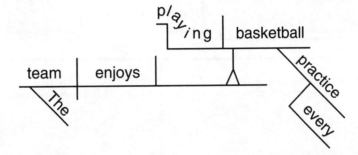

When diagraming infinitives that are used as modifiers, write the diagram as you would for a prepositional phrase.

John walks the dog to help.

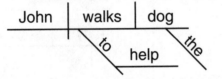

When diagraming infinitives that are used as nouns, the diagram goes in the same place as the noun would.

To be helpful is a scout law.

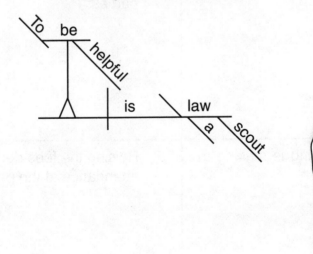

21

Name: _____ Date: _____

Diagraming Gerunds: Practice Activity

Directions: Diagram the following sentences in the space provided. Use the correct form. An example is given.

1. Shala and Kevin like golfing.	5. Learning the violin requires practice.
2. A good report requires planning.	6. Eating vegetables helps your body.
3. Playing the piano has kept Grandma's fingers limber.	7. Sleeping is not allowed at slumber parties.
4. My chore in the morning is making my bed.	8. Raising the fees decreased attendance at the park.

Name: _____ Date: _____

Diagraming Participles: Practice Activity

Directions: Diagram the following sentences in the space provided. Use the correct form. An example is given.

1. The sleeping baby is in the crib. baby ǀ is The / sleeping \ in \ crib the	5. A limping Paulo was sent to the sidelines.
2. Washing the dishes, Dan was very cautious.	6. Ashley, waiting for the bus, dropped her mitten.
3. Eric and Ted will practice at the batting cage.	7. Jamal loaded the washing machine.
4. The leaping dolphin entertained the crowd.	8. Waving goodbye, Kenneth stepped on the plane.

23

Name: _____ Date: _____

Diagraming Gerunds, Participles: Review Activity

Directions: Diagram the following sentences in the space provided. Use the correct form. An example is given.

1. The baking cookies smelled delicious. cookies | smelled \ delicious The / baking	5. The blaring concert hurt Consuela's ears.
2. Exercising is a healthy way to start the day.	6. Jing Mei enjoys walking.
3. By getting home first, Juan had extra chores.	7. Standing on a ladder helps you with washing windows.
4. Joan and Dick dislike washing the car.	8. Holding her bat, Sally swung with all her might.

Name: _____ Date: _____

Diagraming Infinitives: Practice Activity

Directions: Diagram the following sentences in the space provided. Use the correct form. An example is given.

1. Jennifer has many ways to fix her hair.	5. Mrs. Jackson asked to hear from the yearbook staff.
2. Abbie wants to know the capital of Laos.	6. My family hopes to fly to Orlando.
3. Ling and Mario plan to audition for the musical.	7. My group has to finish a mural.
4. Do you want to go to the movies?	8. Ryan finally learned to dive.

Diagraming Predicate Nominatives, Predicate Adjectives

When diagraming predicate nominatives or predicate adjectives, you write the word on the same line as the simple subject and the verb. It is written after the verb. The line dividing the verb from the predicate nominative or predicate adjective does not cross the base line and slants back toward the subject to show the connection.

| subject | verb \ pred. nom. |

Nick is an athlete. (predicate nominative)

Nick | is \ athlete
an

| subject | verb \ pred. adj. |

Carol is tall.   (predicate adjective)

Carol | is \ tall

Name: _____ Date: _____

Diagraming Predicate Nominatives, Predicate Adjectives: Practice Activity 1

Directions: Diagram the following sentences in the space provided. Use the correct form. An example is given.

1. I am a member of the tennis team.	5. The swimming pool looked cool and refreshing.
2. The day seemed sticky after the rain.	6. Kayla will be the representative at the meeting.
3. The dogs are excited at the sight of our cat.	7. The leftovers were dinner on Tuesday.
4. That lady is my mother.	8. Did the class seem quiet in the afternoon?

Name: _____ Date: _____

Diagraming Predicate Nominatives, Predicate Adjectives: Practice Activity 2

Directions: Diagram the following sentences in the space provided. Use the correct form. An example is given.

1. My sister is a cheerleader. sister | is \\ cheerleader \\My \\a	5. The best singers in Chorus are Tom and Alexis.
2. Children should be quiet in the library.	6. We were tired today.
3. Does this book seem boring?	7. Jenny is a good gymnast.
4. Chemistry is my hardest class.	8. The brownies tasted delicious.

Diagraming Compound Sentences

When diagraming compound sentences, each independent clause is diagramed as a sentence. The diagrams are connected by a dotted line with the connecting conjunction written on the horizontal part of the line. The diagrams are connected at the verbs.

Evan ran in the race, but he lost.

My puppy is the runt, but she is cute, and she eats her food.

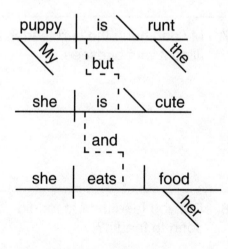

Name: _____ Date: _____

Diagraming Compound Sentences: Practice Activity

Directions: Diagram the following sentences in the space provided. Use the correct form. An example is given.

1. The students reviewed the chapter, because they have a test tomorrow.

2. Michael joined the track team, but he didn't expect to win.

3. Ron and Alec traveled to France, and they sent me a postcard.

4. The rain left big puddles, and the children floated twigs in them.

5. Annie didn't go to ballet class, because she sprained her ankle.

6. Hal's speech ran overtime, so he received a lower grade.

7. My dad hung the bird feeder, and he filled it with birdseed.

8. Did you feed the cat, or did you ask John to feed it?

Diagraming Appositives; There, Where, Here

When diagraming sentences, the appositive is written after the word to which it refers. The appositive is written inside parentheses.

Juanita, the new girl, sits here.

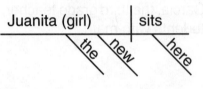

When diagraming sentences with *There, Where,* or *Here* at the beginning of the sentence, those words modify the verb.

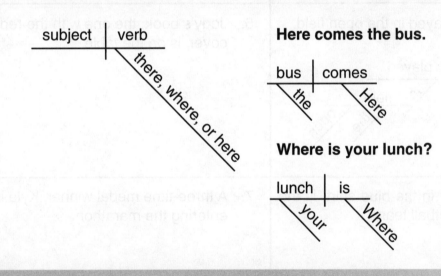

Here comes the bus.

Where is your lunch?

When *there* is not used to modify the verb, it is written on a line above the sentence.

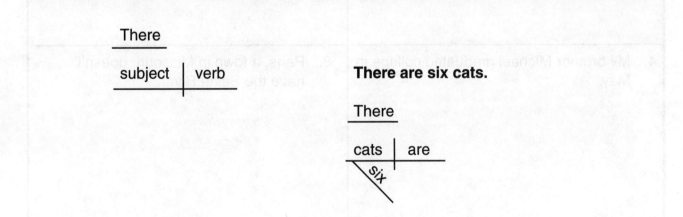

There are six cats.

Name: _____ Date: _____

Diagraming Appositives: Practice Activity

Directions: Diagram the following sentences in the space provided. Use the correct form. An example is given.

1. Mrs. Garcia, the third grade teacher, helps the students with math.	5. Mr. Ichiro's son Troy is my tennis partner.
2. My dog Rusty played in the open field. dog (Rusty) | played My ... in field the open	6. Jody's book, the one with the red cover, is on the table.
3. Kwame, the boy in the blue shirt, is the star of the basketball team.	7. A three-time medal winner, Kyle is entering the marathon.
4. My brother Michael graduated college in May.	8. Paris, a town in Missouri, doesn't have the Seine River.

Name: _____ Date: _____

Diagraming There, Where, Here: Practice Activity

Directions: Diagram the following sentences in the space provided. Use the correct form. An example is given.

1. Here are the books. books | are 　the　　Here	5. There they go.
2. Where are you going?	6. Where can I get a new umbrella?
3. There were two newspapers.	7. Here are the names of the finalists.
4. Here comes the parade!	8. There are the baby bunnies.

Name: _____ Date: _____

Diagraming Subjects, Predicates, Adjectives, Adverbs, Appositives: Review Activity

Directions: Diagram the following sentences in the space provided. Use the correct form. An example is given.

1. The snake slithered quietly.	5. I happily ate the last piece.
2. A big brown bookbag, my brother's, rested on a chair.	6. The rain is pouring outside.
3. The sleepy cat curled up. cat | curled The \ sleepy \ up	7. My sister Carol sings rock music.
4. Six engines pulled the freight train.	8. I sat there during the school play.

Name: _____   Date: _____

Overall Review Activity 1

Directions: Diagram the following sentences in the space provided. Use the correct form. An example is given.

1. Some day Jeff will be a leader.	5. The fall leaves are beautiful, but I need to rake them.
2. LaShonda is a good reader, but she dislikes math.	6. Angel works at the library after school.
3. The tornado blew down buildings.	7. I sometimes ride my bike to the store.
4. Jake hopes to attend scout camp.	8. Matteo has a nearly new skateboard.

Jake | hopes
to attend | camp
scout

Name: _____ Date: _____

Overall Review Activity 2

Directions: Diagram the following sentences in the space provided. Use the correct form. An example is given.

1. Carolyn wants to win the tennis tournament.

5. Morgan likes swimming in the ocean.

```
              swimming
                      in   ocean
                              the
  Morgan | likes
```

2. Elizabeth tried baking bread.

6. The science movie was really boring.

3. Jim's aching feet kept him from the hike.

7. Showering in the morning is a good way to start the day.

4. Peter is polite and considerate.

8. Ashley is class president, and Adam is class treasurer.

Glossary

Adjective: Word that modifies nouns and pronouns. Adjectives tell what kind of, which one, or how many.

Adverb: Word that modifies verbs, adjectives, or other adverbs. Adverbs tell how, where, when, and to what extent.

Appositive: A noun or pronoun that follows a noun or pronoun to give more information.

Appositive Phrase: An appositive in a phrase that explains the noun or pronoun.

Compound Sentence: A sentence with two or more independent clauses.

Direct Object: Receives the action of the verb. It answers the question whom or what.

Gerund: A verb ending in *-ing* and used as a noun.

Indirect Object: Precedes the direct object and tells to whom or to what.

Noun: Names a person, place, thing, or idea.

Participle: A verb used as an adjective.

Predicate: The sentence part that says something about the subject. It contains the verb or verb phrase.

Predicate Adjective: An adjective that follows a linking verb and modifies the subject.

Predicate Noun or Nominative: A noun that follows a linking verb and modifies the subject.

Pronoun: Word that takes the place of a noun.

Sentence: A group of words that express a complete thought; has a subject and a predicate.

Simple Sentence: A sentence with just a subject and a verb.

Subject of a Sentence: A person, place, thing, or idea that the sentence is about.

Verb: Word that expresses action or a state of being.

Answer Keys

**Diagraming Subjects and Predicates: Practice
Activity 1 (page 3)**

1. Grass | grows

2. Dogs | play

3.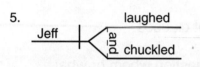
Cats / kittens and | purr

4.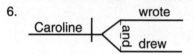
John / I and | raced

5.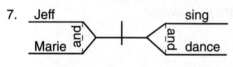
Jeff | laughed and chuckled

6.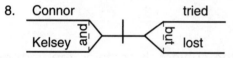
Caroline | wrote and drew

7. Jeff / Marie and | sing and dance

8. Connor / Kelsey and | tried but lost

**Diagraming Subjects and Predicates: Practice
Activity 2 (page 4)**

1. Emily / Erica and | dance and sing

2. Jamal | skates

3. Alexis / Pam and Li | sang

4.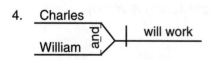
Charles / William and | will work

5.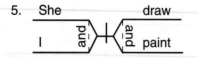
She / I and | draw and paint

6.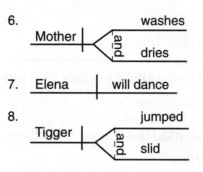
Mother | washes and dries

7. Elena | will dance

8. Tigger | jumped and slid

Diagraming Adjectives: Practice Activity (page 7)

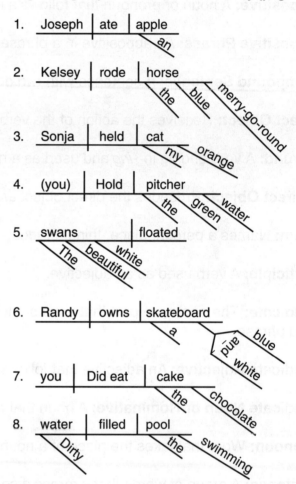

1. Joseph | ate | apple / an

2. Kelsey | rode | horse / the / blue / merry-go-round

3. Sonja | held | cat / my / orange

4. (you) | Hold | pitcher / the / green / water

5. swans | floated / The / beautiful / white

6. Randy | owns | skateboard / a / blue and white

7. you | Did eat | cake / the / chocolate

8. water | filled | pool / Dirty / the / swimming

Diagraming Adverbs: Practice Activity (page 8)

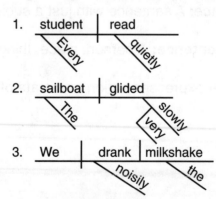

1. student | read / Every / quietly

2. sailboat | glided / The / very slowly

3. We | drank | milkshake / noisily / the

38

4. Jan and Karen | ran outside

5. Josh and Ben | worked quickly

6. (you) | Be very careful

7. Susan | left | room the, quietly very

8. you | Did open | box the, carefully

8. I | ate | cookie the last chip chocolate, happily

Diagraming Subjects, Predicates, Adjectives, Adverbs: Review Activity 1 (page 9)

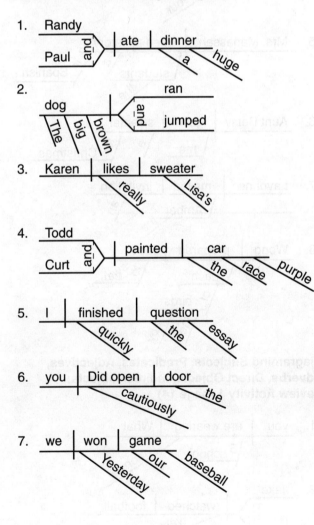

1. Randy and Paul | ate | dinner a huge

2. The big brown dog | ran and jumped

3. Karen | likes | sweater Lisa's, really

4. Todd and Curt | painted | car the race purple

5. I | finished | question the essay, quickly

6. you | Did open | door the, cautiously

7. we | won | game our baseball, Yesterday

Diagraming Subjects, Predicates, Adjectives, Adverbs: Review Activity 2 (page 10)

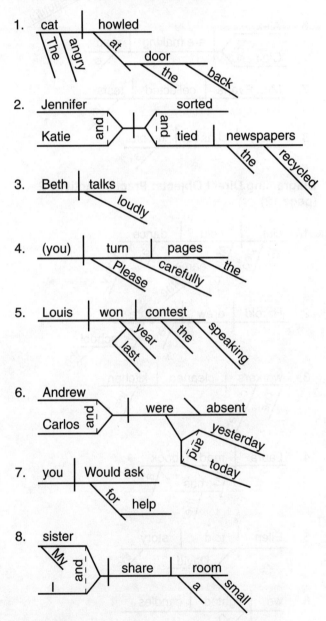

1. The angry cat | howled at door the back

2. Jennifer and Katie | sorted and tied | newspapers the recycled

3. Beth | talks loudly

4. (you) | turn | pages the, Please carefully

5. Louis | won | contest the speaking, year last

6. Andrew and Carlos | were | absent yesterday and today

7. you | Would ask for help

8. My and I sister | share | room a small

Diagraming Direct Objects: Practice Activity 1 (page 11)

1. Mom | made | dinner

2. The state | has | parks many

3. Annie | eats | peanut butter _and_ jelly

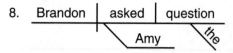

8. Brandon | asked | question / the / Amy

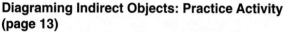

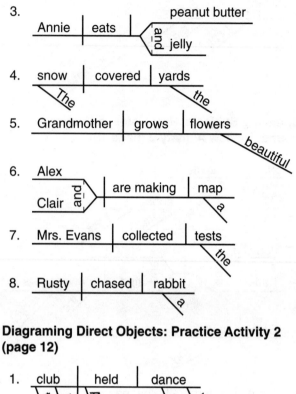

4. snow | covered | yards / The / the

5. Grandmother | grows | flowers / beautiful

6. Alex / Clair _and_ | are making | map / a

7. Mrs. Evans | collected | tests / the

8. Rusty | chased | rabbit / a

Diagraming Direct Objects: Practice Activity 2 (page 12)

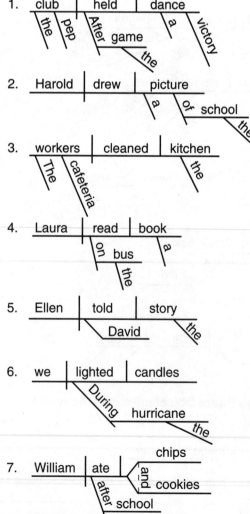

1. club | held | dance / the / pep / After / game / the / a / victory

2. Harold | drew | picture / a / of / school / the

3. workers | cleaned | kitchen / The / cafeteria / the

4. Laura | read | book / on / bus / the / a

5. Ellen | told | story / David / the

6. we | lighted | candles / During / hurricane / the

7. William | ate | chips _and_ cookies / after / school

Diagraming Indirect Objects: Practice Activity (page 13)

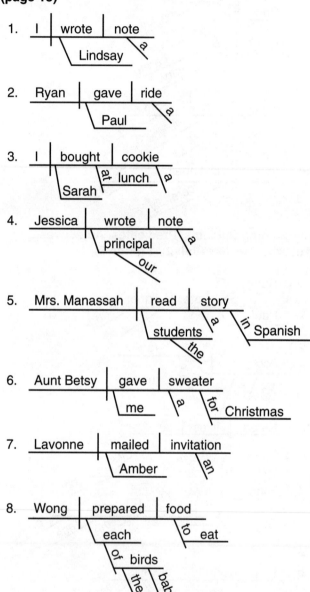

1. I | wrote | note / Lindsay / a

2. Ryan | gave | ride / Paul / a

3. I | bought | cookie / at / lunch / Sarah / a

4. Jessica | wrote | note / principal / our / a

5. Mrs. Manassah | read | story / students / the / a / in / Spanish

6. Aunt Betsy | gave | sweater / me / a / for / Christmas

7. Lavonne | mailed | invitation / Amber / an

8. Wong | prepared | food / each / of / birds / the / baby / to / eat

Diagraming Subjects, Predicates, Adjectives, Adverbs, Direct Objects, Indirect Objects: Review Activity 1 (page 14)

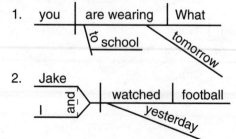

1. you | are wearing | What / to / school / tomorrow

2. Jake / I _and_ | watched | football / yesterday

40

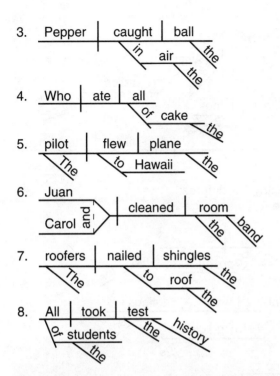

3. Pepper | caught | ball — the — in — air — the

4. Who | ate | all — of — cake — the

5. pilot | flew | plane — The — to — Hawaii — the

6. Juan and Carol | cleaned | room — the — band

7. roofers | nailed | shingles — The — to — roof — the — the

8. All | took | test — of — students — the — the — history

Diagraming Subjects, Predicates, Adjectives, Adverbs, Direct Objects, Indirect Objects: Review Activity 2 (page 15)

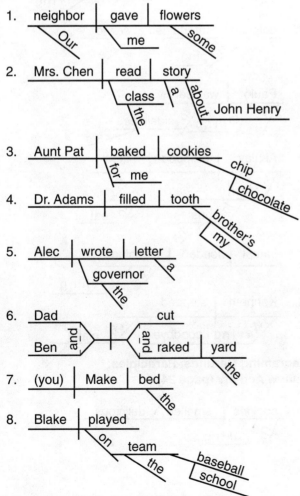

1. neighbor | gave | flowers — Our — me — some

2. Mrs. Chen | read | story — class — a — the — about John Henry

3. Aunt Pat | baked | cookies — for — me — chip — chocolate

4. Dr. Adams | filled | tooth — brother's — my

5. Alec | wrote | letter — governor — a — the

6. Dad and Ben | cut and raked | yard — the

7. (you) | Make | bed — the

8. Blake | played — on — team — the — baseball — school

Diagraming Prepositional Phrases: Practice Activity 1 (page 18)

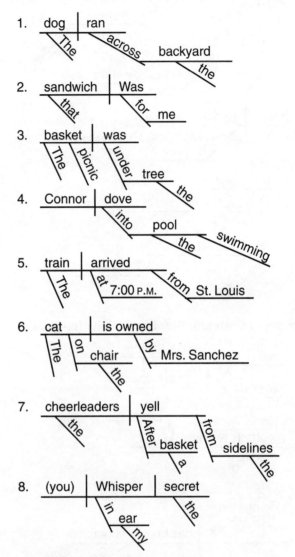

1. dog | ran — The — across — backyard — the

2. sandwich | Was — that — for — me

3. basket | was — The — picnic — under — tree — the

4. Connor | dove — into — pool — the — swimming

5. train | arrived — The — at 7:00 P.M. — from St. Louis

6. cat | is owned — The — on — chair — the — by Mrs. Sanchez

7. cheerleaders | yell — the — After — basket — a — from — sidelines — the

8. (you) | Whisper | secret — in — ear — my — the

Diagraming Prepositional Phrases: Practice Activity 2 (page 19)

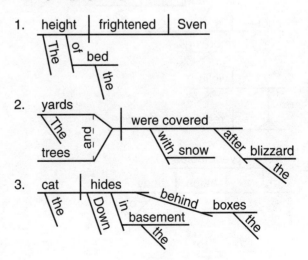

1. height | frightened | Sven — The — of — bed — the

2. yards | were covered — The trees and — with — snow — after — blizzard — the

3. cat | hides — the — Down — in — basement — the — behind — boxes — the

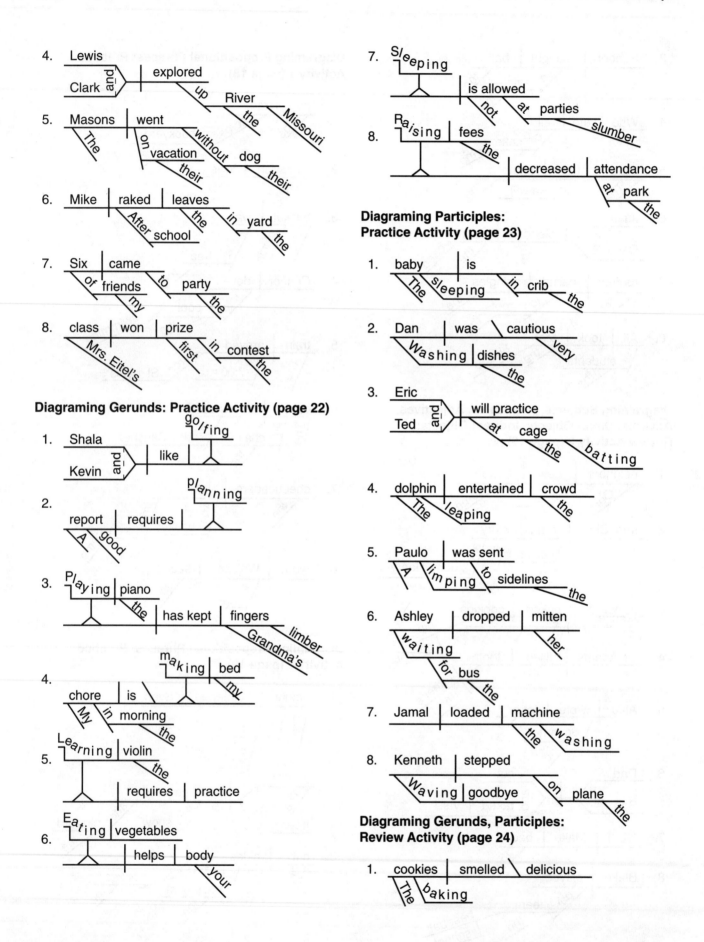

4. Lewis and Clark | explored | up the River Missouri

5. The Masons | went | on vacation without their dog their

6. Mike | raked | the leaves | After school in the yard

7. Six of friends my | came | to the party

8. Mrs. Eitel's class | won | first prize in the contest

Diagraming Gerunds: Practice Activity (page 22)

1. Shala and Kevin | like | golfing

2. A good report | requires | planning

3. Playing the piano | has kept | Grandma's fingers limber

4. My chore | is | making my bed in the morning

5. Learning the violin | requires | practice

6. Eating vegetables | helps | your body

7. Sleeping | is allowed | not at parties slumber

8. Raising the fees | decreased | attendance at the park

Diagraming Participles:
Practice Activity (page 23)

1. The baby sleeping | is | in the crib

2. Dan Washing the dishes | was | cautious very

3. Eric and Ted | will practice | at the batting cage

4. The dolphin leaping | entertained | crowd the

5. Paulo A limping | was sent | to sidelines the

6. Ashley waiting for the bus | dropped | mitten her

7. Jamal | loaded | the washing machine

8. Kenneth Waving goodbye | stepped | on the plane

Diagraming Gerunds, Participles:
Review Activity (page 24)

1. The cookies baking | smelled | delicious

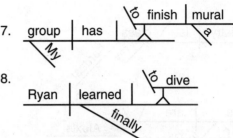

7.

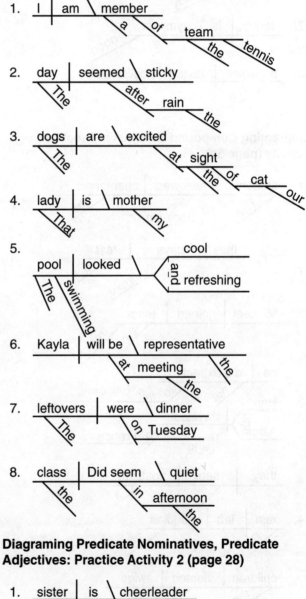

8. Ryan | learned ... to dive ... finally

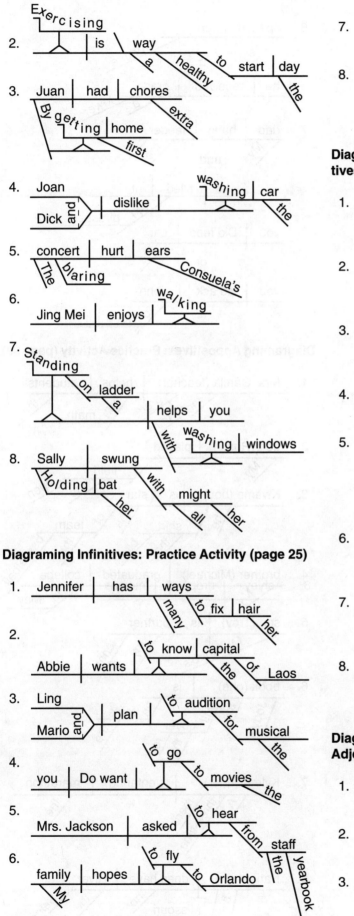

2. Exercising | is \ way ... a / healthy / to start | day / the

3. Juan | had | chores ... By getting | home ... first / extra

4. Joan / Dick and | dislike | washing | car / the

5. concert | hurt | ears ... The / blaring / Consuela's

6. Jing Mei | enjoys | walking

7. Standing ... on | ladder / a ... helps | you ... with washing | windows

8. Sally | swung ... Holding | bat / her ... with / might / all / her

Diagraming Infinitives: Practice Activity (page 25)

1. Jennifer | has | ways ... many / to fix | hair / her

2. Abbie | wants ... to know | capital ... the / of | Laos

3. Ling / Mario and | plan ... to audition ... for | musical / the

4. you | Do want ... to go ... to movies / the

5. Mrs. Jackson | asked ... to hear ... from | staff / the | yearbook

6. family | hopes ... My ... to fly ... to | Orlando

Diagraming Predicate Nominatives, Predicate Adjectives: Practice Activity 1 (page 27)

1. I | am \ member ... a / of | team / the \ tennis

2. day | seemed \ sticky ... The / after | rain / the

3. dogs | are \ excited ... The / at | sight / the / of | cat \ our

4. lady | is \ mother ... That / my

5. pool | looked \ cool and refreshing ... The / swimming

6. Kayla | will be \ representative ... at | meeting / the \ the

7. leftovers | were \ dinner ... The / on | Tuesday

8. class | Did seem \ quiet ... the / in | afternoon / the

Diagraming Predicate Nominatives, Predicate Adjectives: Practice Activity 2 (page 28)

1. sister | is \ cheerleader ... My / a

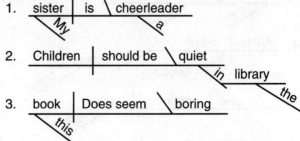

2. Children | should be \ quiet ... in | library / the

3. book | Does seem \ boring ... this

43

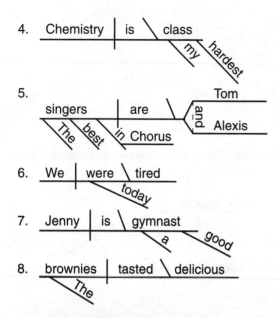

4. Chemistry | is \ class / my \ hardest

5. The singers | are / best in Chorus — and — Tom / Alexis

6. We | were \ tired / today

7. Jenny | is \ gymnast / a \ good

8. The brownies | tasted \ delicious

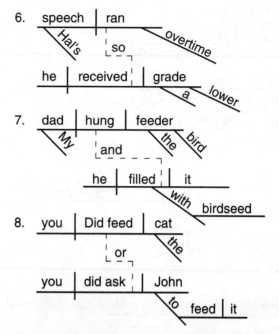

6. Hal's speech | ran \ overtime — so — he | received | grade / a \ lower

7. My dad | hung | feeder \ the \ bird — and — he | filled | it \ with \ birdseed

8. you | Did feed | cat \ the — or — you | did ask | John / to feed | it

Diagraming Compound Sentences: Practice Activity (page 30)

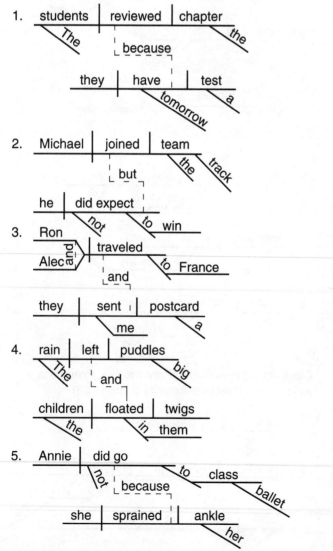

1. The students | reviewed | chapter \ the — because — they | have | test \ a \ tomorrow

2. Michael | joined | team \ the \ track — but — he | did expect \ not / to win

3. Ron / Alec — and — traveled / to France — and — they | sent | postcard / me \ a

4. The rain | left | puddles \ big — and — children | floated | twigs \ the / in \ them

5. Annie | did go \ not / to class \ ballet — because — she | sprained | ankle \ her

Diagraming Appositives: Practice Activity (page 32)

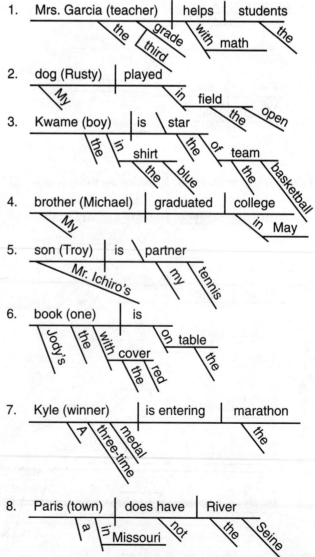

1. Mrs. Garcia (teacher) | helps | students \ the / grade \ the / third \ with \ math

2. My dog (Rusty) | played / in field \ the \ open

3. Kwame (boy) | is \ star \ the / in \ shirt \ the \ blue / of \ team \ the \ basketball

4. My brother (Michael) | graduated | college / in \ May

5. son (Troy) \ Mr. Ichiro's | is \ partner / my \ tennis

6. book (one) \ Jody's \ the \ with \ cover \ the \ red / on \ table \ the

7. Kyle (winner) \ A / three-time \ medal | is entering | marathon \ the

8. Paris (town) / a \ in \ Missouri | does have | River \ not \ the \ Seine

Diagraming There, Where, Here: Practice Activity (page 33)

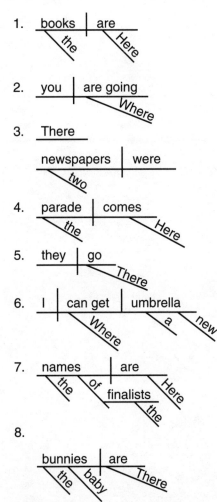

1. books | are / the / Here

2. you | are going / Where

3. There
   newspapers | were / two

4. parade | comes / the / Here

5. they | go / There

6. I | can get | umbrella / Where / a / new

7. names | are / the / of / finalists / Here / the

8.
   bunnies | are / the / baby / There

Diagraming Subjects, Predicates, Adjectives, Adverbs, Appositives: Review Activity (page 34)

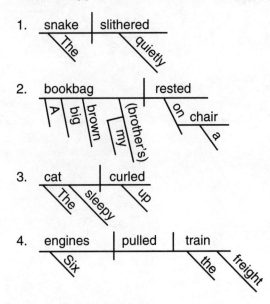

1. snake | slithered / The / quietly

2. bookbag | rested / A / big / brown / (brother's) / my / on / chair / a

3. cat | curled / The / sleepy / up

4. engines | pulled | train / Six / the / freight

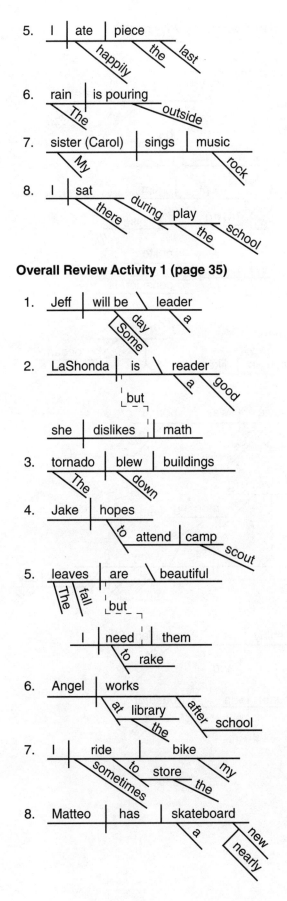

5. I | ate | piece / happily / the / last

6. rain | is pouring / The / outside

7. sister (Carol) | sings | music / My / rock

8. I | sat / there / during | play / the / school

Overall Review Activity 1 (page 35)

1. Jeff | will be \ leader / day / Some / a

2. LaShonda | is \ reader / a / good
   but
   she | dislikes | math

3. tornado | blew | buildings / The / down

4. Jake | hopes / to | attend | camp / scout

5. leaves | are \ beautiful / The / fall
   but
   I | need | them / to | rake

6. Angel | works / at | library / the / after / school

7. I | ride | bike / sometimes / to | store / my / the

8. Matteo | has | skateboard / a / new / nearly

Overall Review Activity 2 (page 36)

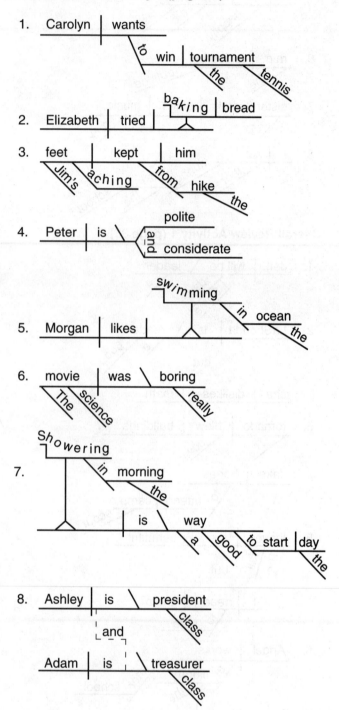

1. Carolyn | wants
       to win | tournament
            the   tennis

2. Elizabeth | tried | baking | bread

3. feet | kept | him
     Jim's aching from hike
                          the

4. Peter | is \ polite
              and
              considerate

5. Morgan | likes | swimming
                     in ocean
                        the

6. movie | was \ boring
   The science   really

7. Showering
       in morning
          the
          is way
          a good to start | day
                             the

8. Ashley | is \ president
                  class
        and
   Adam | is \ treasurer
                class

46